OUR BODIES

DIGESTION

Steve Parker

Raintree

Chicago, Illinois

Titles in the series:
The Brain and Nervous System • Digestion
The Heart, Lungs, and Blood • Reproduction
The Senses • The Skeleton and Muscles

For information address the publisher
Raintree, 100 N. LaSalle, Suite 1200, Chicago, IL 60602

Library of Congress Cataloging-in-Publication Data:

Parker, Steve.
  Digestion / Steve Parker.
     v. cm. -- (Our bodies)
Includes bibliographical references and index.
Contents: The process of digestion -- Dental care -- The stomach -- Digestive problems -- Cleansing the blood.
  ISBN 0-7398-6620-6 (lib. bdg.)
  1. Digestion--Juvenile literature. 2. Digestive organs--Juvenile literature. [1. Digestive system.] I. Title. II. Series.
  QP145.P164 2004
  612.3--dc21

                              2003011337

08 07 06 05 04
10 9 8 7 6 5 4 3 2 1
Printed and bound in China

Picture Acknowledgments
The publisher would like to thank the following for permission to reproduce photographs:
pp. 1,9 Science Photo Library (BSIP Dr. Pichard); p. 4 Corbis (Joel Sartore); p. 5 Corbis (Kevin Fleming); pp. 7, 10 Topham Picturepoint (ImageWorks/Bob Daemmrich); p. 13 bottom Topham Picturepoint (ImageWorks); pp. 14, 33 (bottom) Alamy; p. 15 Science Photo Library (James King-Holmes); p. 17 Science Photo Library (Zephyr); p. 19 Science Photo Library (Prof. P Motta/Department of Anatomy, Univ. La Sapienza, Rome); pp. 21 (bottom), 23 (top), 24 Science Photo Library (Dr. Beergabel/CNRI); p. 23 (bottom) Corbis Digital Stock; p. 25 Nature Picture Library (Duncan McEwan); p. 27 (right) Corbis (Amos Nachoum); p. 29 Science Photo Library (Hattie Young); p. 30 Anthony Blake Photo Library (Gerrit Buntrock); p. 31 Science Photo Libary (Prof. P Motta and T Naguro); p. 33 (top) Science Photo Libary (Zephyr); p. 34 Science Photo Library (Brian Yarvin); p. 37 (left), 39 Science Photo Library (Simon Fraser); p. 38 Science Photo Library (Dr. Kari Lounatmaa); p. 40 Rex Features (Chris Martin Bahr); p. 41 Science Photo Library (CNRI); pp. 43, 44, 45 Science Photo Library (Maximilian Stock Ltd); p. 45 (top) Topham Picturepoint (ImageWorks/Jacksonville Journal Courier).

Front cover (main image) Topham Picturepoint (ImageWorks/Bob Daemmrich)
Front cover (inset) Science Photo Library (BSIP Dr. Pichard)

CONTENTS

INTRODUCTION

Eat up!

Most people eat about ten times their own body weight in food each year. In a large adult, this annual food intake may weigh almost one ton. Of course, the body does not gain this huge amount of weight each year. Instead, the foods are used in many different ways.

Vast areas of land are used to produce our food through growing crops and raising livestock. The food business employs millions of people.

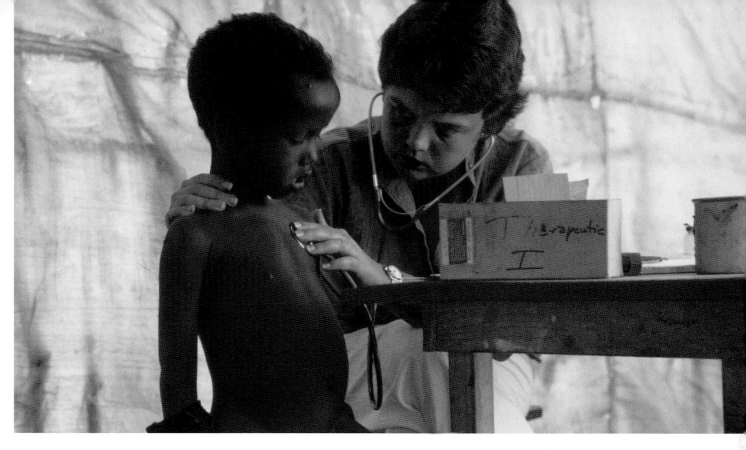

Why the body needs food

Some parts of food are used for energy, which allows you to move, talk, walk, run, and carry out all other activities. This energy also powers the body's inner processes, such as breath and heartbeat, which continue every minute of every day. Some of the substances in food are used for growth, and others for maintenance and repair. Every day, parts of the body such as the skin wear out or suffer from injuries too small to notice. This is normal, and the parts are replaced and repaired without our realizing it. If the body suffers from a bigger injury, the repair process is much more obvious.

Some parts of food are not used at all. They pass through the body and are excreted in a form that is hardly altered.

About one third of people in the world—over two billion—do not have enough food to stay well nourished. Lack of food brings many kinds of health problems, including an increased risk of infections.

Food and health

Food is more than simply fuel for energy and **nutrients** for growth, maintenance, and repair. Some substances in food are needed for good health. All of the foods that a person eats are called a **diet.** It is important that a diet has many different kinds of food, all in the right proportions. A diet that provides the body with all its nutrients and keeps it healthy is known as a balanced diet. Maintaining a balanced diet is one of the most important things you can do to keep your body in good health.

THE PROCESS OF DIGESTION

Eating and digestion

In **digestion** the body breaks food down into tiny pieces, far too small to see, so that they can be taken into and used by the body. But this is only part of the whole process of taking in food. First, the food is put into the body by biting, chewing, and swallowing. This process is called ingestion. The swallowed food passes into a long passageway through the body, the **digestive tract** (shown on the following pages). Here, the food is broken apart by physical methods such as squeezing and by chemical methods in which powerful juices are added to it to make it dissolve, or turn into a soupy liquid. This physical and chemical attack on food is called digestion.

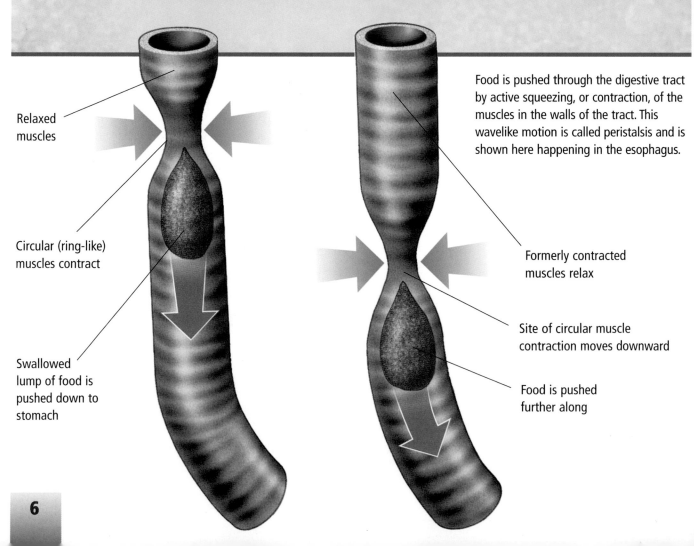

Relaxed muscles

Circular (ring-like) muscles contract

Swallowed lump of food is pushed down to stomach

Food is pushed through the digestive tract by active squeezing, or contraction, of the muscles in the walls of the tract. This wavelike motion is called peristalsis and is shown here happening in the esophagus.

Formerly contracted muscles relax

Site of circular muscle contraction moves downward

Food is pushed further along

Taken into the body

The next stage is absorption, when digested substances are small enough to pass or seep through the lining of the digestive tract. They enter the blood and are spread around the body. Some parts of food are left in the tract. Eventually these leftover and undigested remains leave the body at the end of the tract. This is called elimination.

Muscle power

When food is swallowed, it does not "fall" down the inside of the body. Rather, the body is full of many parts that are squashed tightly together. This squeezing presses on the digestive tract, like a hose squashed flat. Food must be pushed along the tract by force. This is done by muscles in the walls of the tract, which squeeze with a wavelike motion that travels along the tract, pushing the foods within. The wavelike motion is known as **peristalsis.** You do not notice peristalsis when it is happening in your body.

ANIMAL VERSUS HUMAN

In the digestive tract of humans and animals, the squeezing motion of peristalsis is strong enough to push food and drinks not only downward, but upward. When a giraffe stoops to drink, peristalsis pushes the water from its mouth up its neck to its body—a height of over 6.5 feet (almost 2 meters).

Parts of the digestive tract

About ten body parts work together to take in and digest food and then absorb the resulting **nutrients.** These parts are known as the **digestive system.** Most of them form a passageway through the body, the **digestive tract.** This begins in the mouth, where teeth bite and chew food and the tongue tastes it and moves it around when chewing. Parts called salivary glands around the mouth add a watery liquid, **saliva** (spit), to make the food soft and squishy. Swallowed food passes through the throat and down a tube, the esophagus, into the stomach. This is a stretchy bag that holds a whole meal of food and drink and partly digests it to form a mushy "soup."

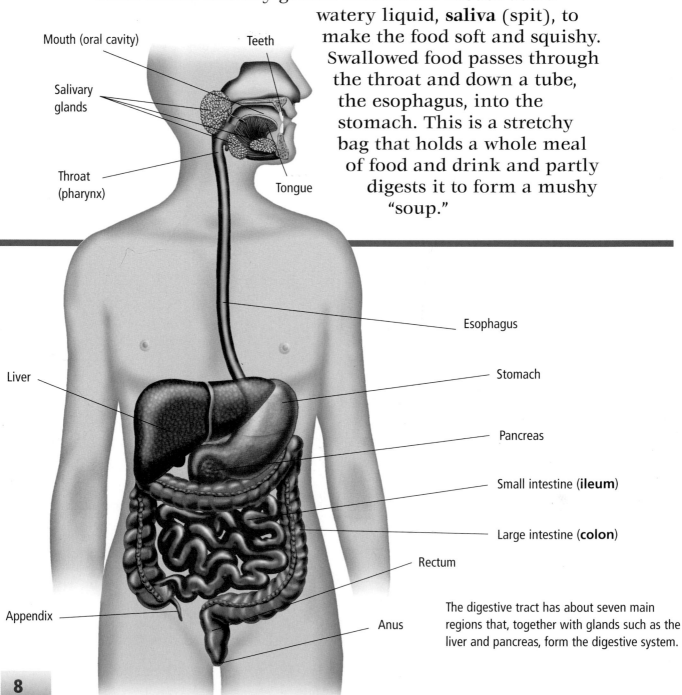

Mouth (oral cavity)

Teeth

Salivary glands

Throat (pharynx)

Tongue

Liver

Esophagus

Stomach

Pancreas

Small intestine (**ileum**)

Large intestine (**colon**)

Rectum

Appendix

Anus

The digestive tract has about seven main regions that, together with glands such as the liver and pancreas, form the digestive system.

The substance barium shows up as pale areas on an X-ray image. Here, it has been swallowed as part of a medical test and fills the loops and coils of the small intestine.

Intestines, small and large

From the stomach, digested food oozes along a very long tube, the small intestine, that is folded and coiled within the body. This is where **digestion** continues and where most nutrients are absorbed. The tract's next part is the large intestine, where a few last nutrients and water are absorbed from the contents. The leftovers are stored in the next part, the rectum, before they leave from the end of the tract, the anus.

More parts of the system

Two parts are not in the digestive tract, but they are in the digestive system: the liver and the pancreas. The pancreas makes juices that flow along a short tube and empty into the small intestine where they help to digest food. The liver makes another fluid, bile, that also flows into the small intestine to help digest certain foods. The liver also receives the blood that has absorbed the nutrients from the intestines. It stores some nutrients, changes others into different forms, and releases others around the body when they are needed.

Try this!

The whole digestive tract is more than 26 feet (8 meters) long. Use a tape measure to cut a piece of thick string or rope to this length. Can you fold and coil it up so it would fit into your body—without getting it tangled?

9

FIRST STOP FOR FOOD

Bite and chew

The mouth is the first part of the **digestive tract.** The front teeth bite pieces off large food items and the back teeth chew them. (Teeth are shown in more detail on pages 12 and 13.) When chewing, the lips seal together so that bits of food do not fall out, while the cheeks bulge to hold food as it is squished between the back teeth.

The tongue's many tasks

The tongue tastes food so that we know what we are eating. This gives us pleasure when we enjoy a meal. It can also be helpful because bitter or strange tastes may warn that a food is rotten or "bad" in some way. The tongue's roughened upper surface moves food around during chewing so that the whole mouthful is crushed and soft. The tongue also helps shift pieces of food that get stuck in the teeth and licks pieces of food off the lips.

All parts of the mouth are involved in eating. The front teeth bite, the lips grip and pull in the bitten-off pieces and then close, and the tongue moves the pieces around for chewing by the rear teeth.

Top Tips

Make time for mealtimes. Chew each mouthful well and savor the flavor. Eating in a hurry means that food is not chewed properly, so the body cannot digest and use all of its **nutrients.** Also, swallowing partially chewed food can cause pain or even choking.

Making food moist

As food is chewed, it is mixed with watery **saliva,** which is made in parts around the mouth called salivary glands. Saliva flows from each gland along a short tube, the salivary duct, into the mouth. The six glands make more than one quart (one liter) of saliva each day, which is mostly stored until eating begins, when it flows into the mouth. Saliva makes chewed food moist and slippery for easy swallowing. It also contains body chemicals called **enzymes** that begin to digest certain foods even before they are swallowed (see page 30).

Saliva makes foods moist, soft, and easily swallowed. It is made in three pairs of salivary glands. On each side of the face, left and right, there is a parotid salivary gland just below and in front of the ear, a submandibular salivary gland inside the lower jaw, and a sublingual salivary gland under the tongue and floor of the mouth.

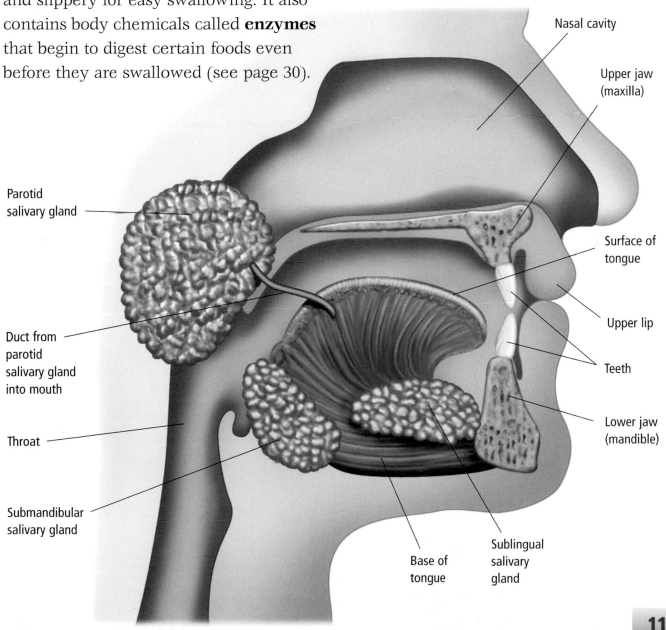

Nasal cavity

Upper jaw (maxilla)

Surface of tongue

Upper lip

Teeth

Lower jaw (mandible)

Parotid salivary gland

Duct from parotid salivary gland into mouth

Throat

Submandibular salivary gland

Base of tongue

Sublingual salivary gland

THE TEETH

Two sets of teeth

The human body has two sets of teeth. The first set of 20 teeth grows from about birth to three years of age. They are called baby teeth, milk teeth, or the deciduous dentition. At about six years of age, the first teeth begin to fall out naturally and are replaced by the second set, called adult teeth, or the permanent dentition. Most people have 32 teeth. In some people the rearmost, or "wisdom teeth" never grow above the gum. Many people have their wisdom teeth removed.

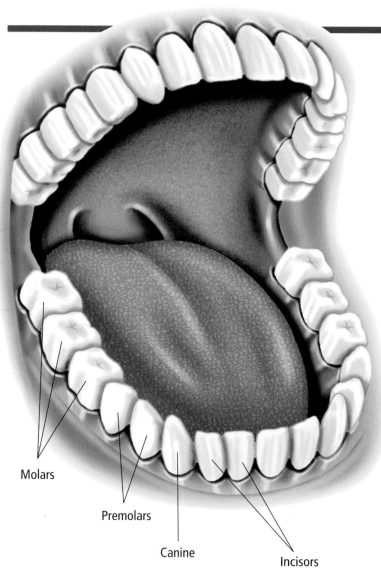

Molars

Premolars

Canine

Incisors

Most adults have 32 teeth. In each half (left and right) of each jaw (upper and lower) there are two incisors, one canine, two premolars, and three molars. However, in some people, certain teeth never appear, or "erupt." They stay small and undeveloped within the jawbone, under the gums.

Types of teeth

There are four kinds of teeth, in both the first and second sets. At the front of the mouth are incisors, with straight, sharp edges like small shovels. These are designed to nibble, bite, and slice off chunks of food. Behind them are canines ("eye teeth"), which are taller and more pointed and used for tearing up tough foods. Next are the wider premolars, which are used for squashing and crushing. At the rear of the mouth are the molars, or cheek teeth, which are even broader and used for the most powerful chewing.

A tooth (this is a molar with two roots) is fixed by glue-like cementum into its socket in the jaw bone.

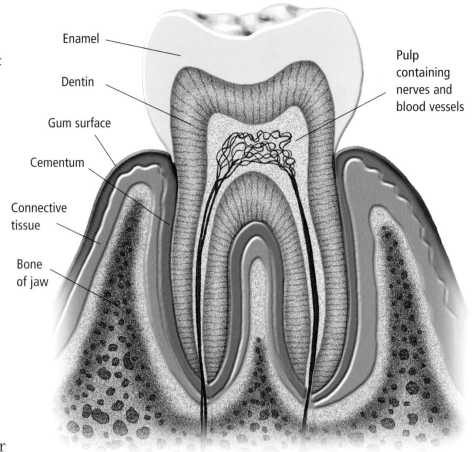

Enamel

Dentin

Gum surface

Cementum

Connective tissue

Bone of jaw

Pulp containing nerves and blood vessels

Inside a tooth

A tooth has two main parts: the upper crown, which shows above the gum, and the lower root, which is fixed firmly into the jawbone. No substance in the body is harder than **enamel,** which forms the whitish outer covering of the crown. It must withstand years of rubbing, scraping, and wear. Under it is a layer of slightly softer but still very tough dentin. This acts as a cushion to absorb the tremendous forces of crunching into hard foods. In the middle of the tooth is dental pulp. This contains blood vessels that nourish the outer layers and **nerves** that feel if the tooth is biting too hard or has other problems.

ANIMAL VERSUS HUMAN

In some animals the different types of teeth vary much more in size than they do in humans. In a lion or tiger, the canine teeth are very long and sharp so that the cat can jab into and tear up its prey.

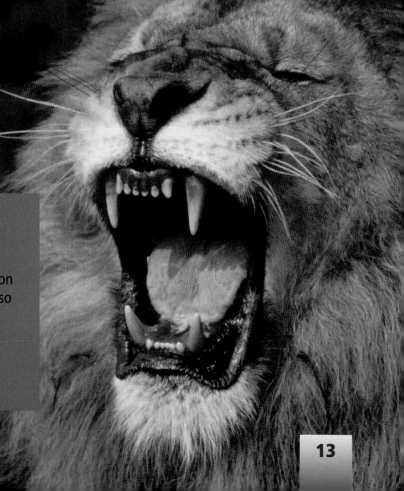

DENTAL CARE

Smile at the dentist

When did you last visit the dentist? Regular dental checkups are important for many reasons. The dentist looks around the whole mouth to make sure there are no health problems—not only with the teeth, but with the gums, tongue, and other parts. Then, each tooth is checked to make sure it is clean and healthy and growing straight. Some people naturally have stronger, healthier teeth than others, but everyone needs a regular dental checkup.

Various designs of orthodontic appliances help the teeth to grow straight and evenly spaced.

Dental decay

The dentist looks for chips or cracks in the teeth and for patches that might be soft or have holes. This could be a sign of dental decay, also known as caries. It happens when teeth are not cleaned properly or often enough. Old pieces of food on and between the teeth rot as they are "eaten" by tiny microbes called bacteria. The bacteria make chemicals—acids—that destroy the tooth's **enamel** and cause pits and holes known as cavities. The tooth becomes weak, and if the decay reaches the pulp, it affects

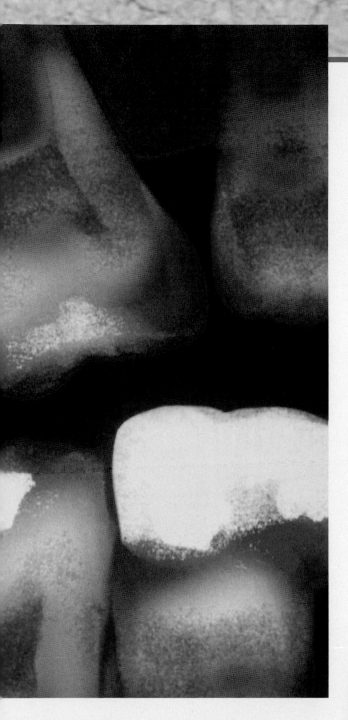

This computer-colored dental X-ray shows teeth repaired with amalgam filling, which shows up bright white.

the **nerves** and causes toothaches. Sometimes the dentist takes an X-ray that shows the inside of the tooth. This reveals decay that cannot be seen clearly from the outside.

Keeping teeth clean

To prevent dental decay and toothache, it is important to clean teeth and keep gums healthy, as advised by the dentist or oral hygienist. This is usually done in the morning, after main meals, and before bed at night. The most important methods are to brush the teeth thoroughly with toothpaste and to floss the gaps between the teeth. The dentist or oral hygienist will show you the best method. A mouthwash may also help, not only for teeth, but also for the gums and the rest of the mouth. In addition to cleaning teeth, all of these methods help to get rid of "bad breath," or halitosis, which can be caused by pieces of decaying food.

Try this!

Have you used "disclosing" mouthwash or tablets? Ask your pharmacist or dentist. Used according to the instructions, they show, or "disclose," areas that are not clean by making them a certain color. This will help you brush your teeth better in the future!

EATING A MEAL

Mmmm—smells good!

As you start to eat, your **digestive system** is busy throughout most of your body preparing for the meal ahead. Even smelling the food before eating makes your salivary glands pour their **saliva** into your mouth, ready to moisten the food when chewing. This is why we sometimes say a meal "smells mouth-watering."

Chew and swallow

After a mouthful of food is chewed into a soft paste, it can be swallowed safely in small lumps called boluses. We swallow hundreds of times daily, and we rarely think about this complex action unless it goes wrong—when we cough or even choke. Swallowing

Four stages in swallowing show how muscle activity begins with the tongue and moves down the throat into the upper esophagus.

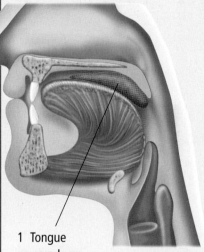

1 Tongue presses lump of food (bolus) to upper rear of mouth

2 Tongue forces food down into throat

3 Epiglottis folds over entrance to windpipe

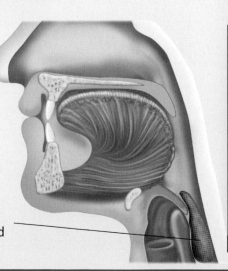

4 Upper esophagus "grabs" food from throat

Try this!

Look in a mirror as you swallow. See how muscles move to push food down into the throat and esophagus in your neck, through **peristalsis.**

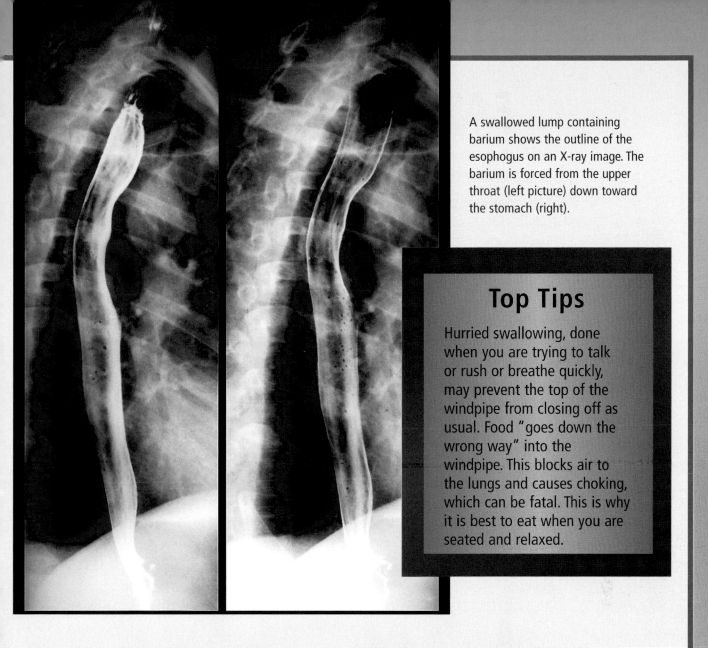

A swallowed lump containing barium shows the outline of the esophogus on an X-ray image. The barium is forced from the upper throat (left picture) down toward the stomach (right).

Top Tips

Hurried swallowing, done when you are trying to talk or rush or breathe quickly, may prevent the top of the windpipe from closing off as usual. Food "goes down the wrong way" into the windpipe. This blocks air to the lungs and causes choking, which can be fatal. This is why it is best to eat when you are seated and relaxed.

begins when the tongue pushes a lump of food to the rear of the mouth. As the food touches the rear of the mouth, upper throat, and base of the tongue, it begins a reflex, or automatic body action. The base of the tongue pushes the lump down into the throat and into the top of the esophagus. Waves of muscle action "catch" the lump and push it downward toward the stomach.

Down the right way

At the bottom of the throat, the opening to the windpipe (trachea), which leads to the lungs, is just in front of the opening to the esophagus. When swallowing, muscles in the throat and neck raise the top of the windpipe and lower a flap, called the epiglottis, just above it so that the two press together. These two actions close the windpipe, which means food has to go down the throat, rather than staying in the windpipe.

THE STOMACH

"Down the hatch"

As food leaves your mouth, it begins a very long journey—about 26 feet (8 meters) in distance and 24 hours in time. Within a few seconds, the mushy, chewed food is pushed down the esophagus into the stomach, a J-shaped bag behind the lower ribs on the left side. The empty stomach is smaller than a fist, but it can quickly stretch to hold more than 1.5 quarts (1.5 liters) of food and drink.

Esophagus

Double digestion

The stomach continues the physical and chemical breakdown of food that began in the mouth. The stomach wall contains three layers of muscles, and these make it squirm and churn and squeeze the food inside, turning it into a mushy soup called chyme.

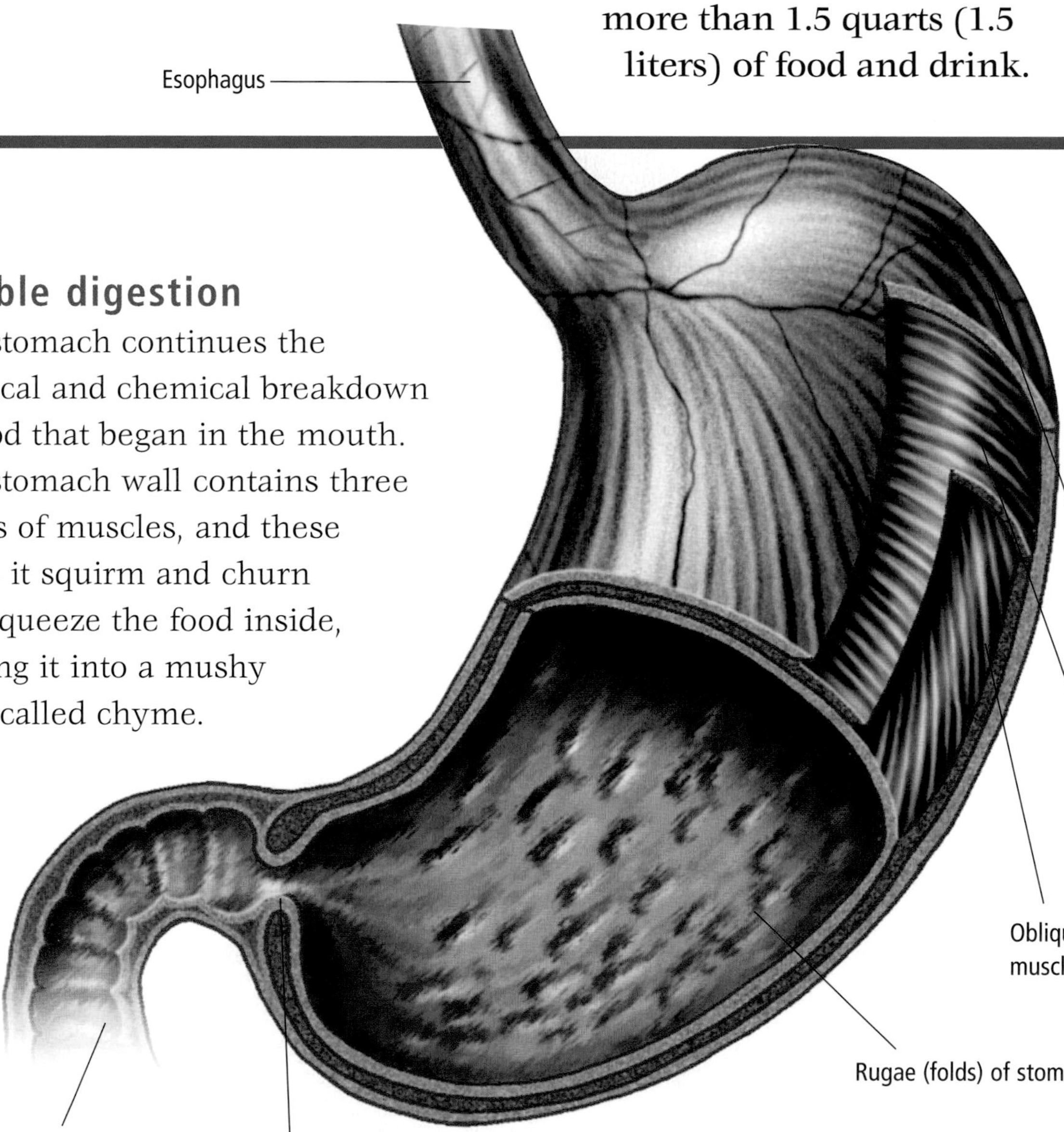

Longitudinal muscle layer

Circular muscle layer

Oblique muscle layer

Rugae (folds) of stomach lining

Duodenum (first part of small intestine)

Pyloric sphincter

The stomach wall's layers of muscles allow it to squeeze food powerfully. The exit from the stomach is through a ring of muscle, the pyloric sphincter.

The stomach's inner lining also makes powerful digestive chemicals, called gastric juices, that dissolve various substances in the food. The juices include a powerful acid, hydrochloric acid, and a variety of **enzymes** (see page 30). The juices also help to kill any harmful germs that were swallowed with the food. Although the stomach is full of these powerful juices, it does not digest itself from the inside out. It has a thick layer of slime-like **mucus** that coats and protects its inner lining.

A long stay

Food usually stays in the stomach for at least one hour. If the meal contained lots of fatty foods, the stay is usually longer, up to four hours, because fats take a long time to break apart.

MICRO BODY

The inner lining of the stomach, called the gastric epithelium, is dotted with thousands of tiny openings leading into holes called gastric pits. Various **cells** down the sides of these pits and at their bases make a variety of substances, including acid, enzymes, and **hormones** to control **digestion.** They also make thick, sticky mucus to protect the lining from its own digestive products.

This microscopic view of the stomach lining looks straight down into several gastric pits, showing some of the cells lining their walls. In life these would be covered by mucus.

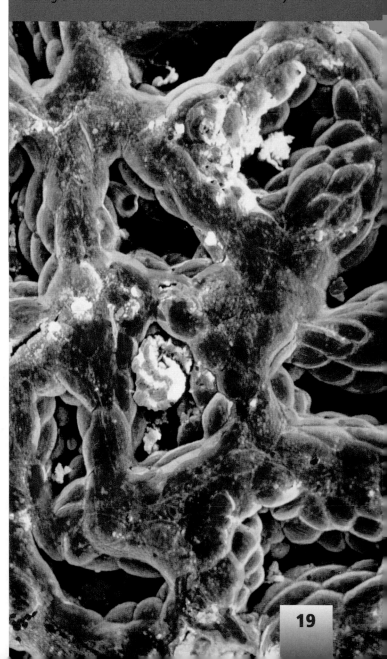

THE SMALL INTESTINE

The longest part

The small intestine is by far the longest part of the **digestive tract,** at about 20 ft (6 m), but also the narrowest, at only 1.6 in. (4 cm) wide. It is looped, folded, and coiled into the lower part of the main body, the **abdomen,** and consists of three sections. First is the **duodenum,** about 10 in. (25 cm) long, which joins at its upper end to the stomach. It leads to the middle section, the **jejunum,** which is about 6.5 ft (2 m) long. Third is the **ileum,** 11.5 ft (3.5 m) in length. The ileum leads into the large intestine, in the lower right of the abdomen.

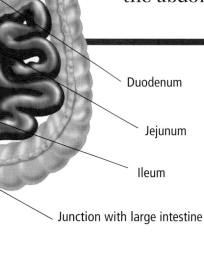

Liver

Exit from stomach

Stomach

Duodenum

Jejunum

Ileum

Junction with large intestine

The small intestine is "framed" by the large one. The exact length of each section of the small intestine—duodenum, jejunum, and ileum—and the layout of its loops and bends within the center of the abdomen vary from person to person.

A huge area

Like the stomach lining, the small intestine lining makes powerful **enzyme**-containing juices to break food into ever-smaller pieces. It also receives digestive juices from the pancreas and liver (see pages 26–29), which also help the breakdown.

Top Tips

As the body digests a meal, extra amounts of blood flow to the stomach, intestines, and other parts. This means less blood is available for other body parts, such as muscles. This is why it is wise to avoid too much activity or exercise, such as playing sports, right after a meal.

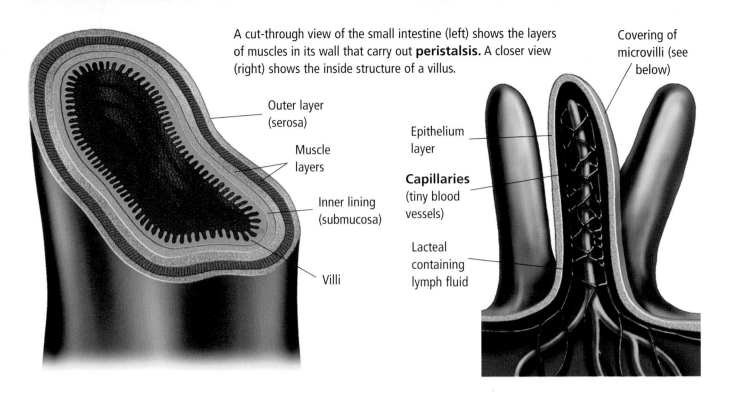

A cut-through view of the small intestine (left) shows the layers of muscles in its wall that carry out **peristalsis.** A closer view (right) shows the inside structure of a villus.

Outer layer (serosa)

Muscle layers

Inner lining (submucosa)

Villi

Covering of microvilli (see below)

Epithelium layer

Capillaries (tiny blood vessels)

Lacteal containing lymph fluid

The small intestine's lining is rippled into folds called plicae. These have thousands of tiny finger-like projections called **villi.** Each villus is about .04 in. (1 mm) long, and each has thousands of even tinier finger-like microvilli. The plicae, villi, and microvilli give the small intestine a huge surface—bigger than the area of five single beds—to take in, or absorb, the greatest amounts of digested **nutrients** from food.

Carried away

Nutrients pass from the sloppy liquid inside the small intestine, through the inner lining, into tiny tubes, or blood vessels, within the intestine wall. The blood carries them away to the liver. Another fluid, **lymph,** flows slowly through its own tiny vessels in the small intestine wall. It also absorbs nutrients, as shown on page 36.

MICRO BODY

Each fingerlike villus (shown above) has a covering of many thousands of even tinier microvilli. These are also shaped like fingers, but each one is only a few thousandths of one millimeter long. Nutrients pass into the microvilli and seep inward to the interior of the villus, to the blood and lymph vessels there.

Microvilli (red) cover the surface of a villus (blue area below) and project into the space within the small intestine (yellow).

The large intestine

After the small intestine, or small bowel, comes the large intestine, also called the large bowel or **colon.** It is about two and a half to three inches (six to seven centimeters) across, but shorter than the small intestine. It passes up the right side of the **abdomen,** across below the liver and stomach, down the left side, and then curves in an S shape to the lower middle of the abdomen.

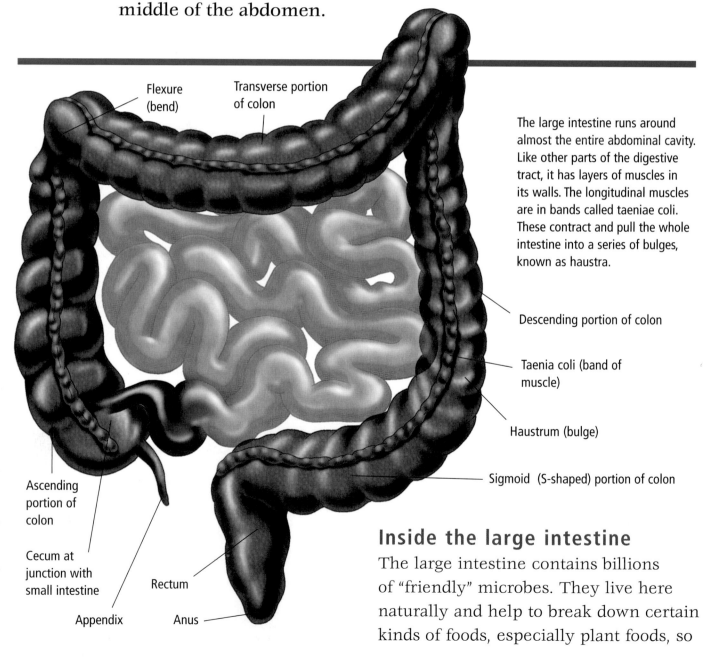

Flexure (bend)

Transverse portion of colon

The large intestine runs around almost the entire abdominal cavity. Like other parts of the digestive tract, it has layers of muscles in its walls. The longitudinal muscles are in bands called taeniae coli. These contract and pull the whole intestine into a series of bulges, known as haustra.

Descending portion of colon

Taenia coli (band of muscle)

Haustrum (bulge)

Ascending portion of colon

Cecum at junction with small intestine

Rectum

Appendix

Anus

Sigmoid (S-shaped) portion of colon

Inside the large intestine

The large intestine contains billions of "friendly" microbes. They live here naturally and help to break down certain kinds of foods, especially plant foods, so

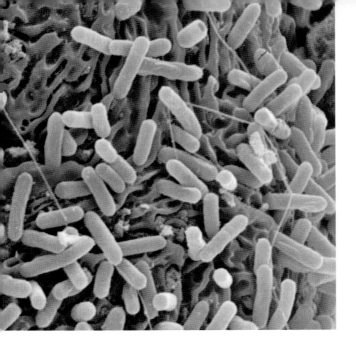

Millions of rod-shaped bacteria, known as *Escherischia coli*, are a normal part of the large intestine's contents.

The last stop

At the end of the large intestine, the leftover and undigested contents, called feces, pass into the last main part of the tract. This is the rectum, which is about 6 inches (15 centimeters) long. The feces stay here until it is convenient to remove them from the body. This is done by squeezing the muscles of the abdomen to push the feces through the loosened ring of muscle at the end of the tract, called the anus.

that the body can absorb the **nutrients.** The large intestine also absorbs much of the water from the leftover digested food, turning it into squishy brown lumps called **feces,** or bowel movements.

The appendix

The appendix is a small part of the **digestive tract,** about the size of a little finger. It is at the junction of the small and large intestines, in the lower right of the abdomen. The appendix is hollow inside and links to the main digestive tract, but it does not lead anywhere and does not seem to have a role in the digestive system. Sometimes digestive waste gets stuck inside and causes swelling and pain, known as appendicitis. In serious cases of appendicitis, the appendix must be surgically removed.

ANIMAL VERSUS HUMAN

The human digestive tract may seem quite long, at more than 26 feet (8 meters). But an animal called the manatee, or sea-cow, has a digestive tract more than 98 feet (30 meters) long! This peaceful mammal lives in warm, shallow water near the coast. It feeds on many kinds of water-plants such as sea-grasses, which take a long time to digest, and can eat more than 265 pounds (120 kilograms) of plant food each day.

DIGESTIVE PROBLEMS

Germs and allergies

Tiny, harmful microbes called germs are almost everywhere—even on clean-looking foods. Normally the stomach's powerful acids and juices kill them. Occasionally, they cause digestive infection, or "food poisoning." Some people are especially sensitive, or allergic, to certain foods, such as nuts or shellfish. This can cause problems in the **digestive system** and elsewhere in the body.

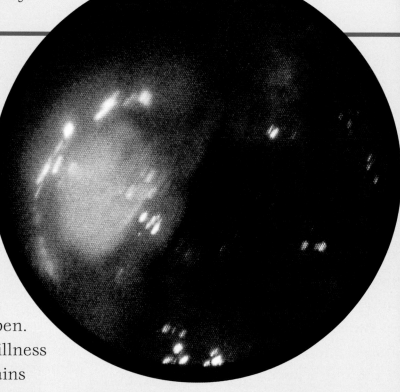

Swallowing in reverse

In some cases the **digestive tract** gets rid of food by reversing its wave-like muscle movements, known as **peristalsis.** The waves start in the stomach and travel up to the throat to eject the food from the mouth in a process called vomiting, or throwing up. Nausea is the feeling that this might happen. Vomiting may happen during an illness or if food is bad or rotten or contains harmful substances.

A view through a flexible, telescope-like endoscope inserted down the throat into the stomach shows an ulcer—the pale oval area. It is like an open sore in the stomach lining.

Aches and pains

Pains in the abdomen are often called stomachaches. However, the stomach is high in the **abdomen,** behind the lower left ribs, so pain from lower down is more likely to be intestinal. General swelling, inflammation, and pain in the stomach and intestines, are

Some fungi, like these fly agaric "toadstools," have bright colors that warn they are poisonous. However, some plain brown or gray fungi can also be deadly.

Top Tips

It is never worth taking a chance by eating food that could be harmful or even deadly. It is wise to wash dirt and germs off fresh or unwrapped foods, to avoid foods from containers that are dented or cracked, and to check with an expert about picked foods such as berries.

usually caused by germs or toxins (poisonous substances) in foods. This is called gastroenteritis. It usually passes as the body defeats the problem, but in certain cases, medicine is needed. An ulcer is a sore or raw area in the lining of the stomach or **duodenum** (first part of the small intestine) that causes pain and, in serious cases, may bleed.

Sometimes digested foods pass through the intestines too quickly and emerge "loose" with lots of fluid, a condition known as diarrhea. The leftovers may also become too compacted and hard and cannot move easily through the last part of the tract, which is a condition known as constipation.

THE LIVER

Hundreds of tasks

Blood from the intestines, rich in **nutrients** from digested food, flows to the body's largest inner organ, the liver. This is in the upper right of the **abdomen,** with most of its bulk behind the lower right ribs. The reddish-brown, smooth-surfaced, wedge-shaped liver has more than two hundred different tasks, mainly to do with metabolism (body chemistry). It breaks down some nutrients, builds up others, stores some until needed, and releases others when their levels in the blood fall too low.

In particular, the liver breaks down harmful substances into harmless ones, a process known as detoxification. For example, the liver detoxifies the alcohol in alcoholic drinks so that some of its harmful effects eventually wear off. However, alcohol gradually damages the liver, causing scarring, or cirrhosis, so that the liver is no longer able to work properly.

Hepatic ducts

Left lobe

Stomach

Right lobe

Clumps of hepatic lobules (see right)

Falciform ligament

Gallbladder

Pancreas

The liver is divided into a larger right lobe and smaller left lobe by the sheet-like falciform ligament.

Accessory pancreatic duct

Main pancreatic duct

Cystic duct

Common bile duct

Duodenum

Sugar and starch

One of the liver's main tasks is to control the level of blood sugar, or **glucose.** This is the main energy source for all body processes. If a digested meal contains plenty of glucose, the liver converts this into body starch and stores it. As the glucose is used and its blood level falls, the liver changes some body starch into glucose and releases this into the blood. The control is carried out by **hormones** (see page 28).

The liver contains thousands of six-sided units called hepatic lobules, each about .04 inches (one millimeter) across. Inside each lobule are many layers of hepatic cells and branches of tiny vessels.

Small branches of hepatic artery and **vein** (blood vessels)

Sheets and clumps of hepatocytes (hepatic cells)

Tiny branches of hepatic duct (collecting bile)

Gallbladder and bile

One of the liver's products is a yellowish fluid called bile. It contains many unwanted substances, including bilirubin, from the breakdown of old, worn-out red blood **cells.** Bile is stored in a small bag, the gallbladder, tucked under the liver. After eating, it flows along the bile duct into the small intestine. Bile helps the **digestion** of fatty foods in the intestine.

ANIMAL VERSUS HUMAN

The human liver weighs a little more than three pounds (under 2 kilograms). The world's biggest fish, the whale shark, has a liver that weighs over a ton—it is the size of a small car and about one-fifth of the shark's total body weight. The liver is very oil-rich with stored nutrients and helps the shark to float easily.

Juices and ducts

The pancreas is a long, pale, slim part in the upper left **abdomen,** mostly behind the stomach. Like the liver, it is part of the **digestive system** but not of the **digestive tract.** It makes powerful digestive fluids, called pancreatic juices, that flow along a tube, the pancreatic duct, into the small intestine. Each day the pancreas makes about 1.6 quarts (1.5 liters) of juices. They contain many body chemicals called **enzymes,** as described on p. 30. These attack and break down different food substances in the small intestine.

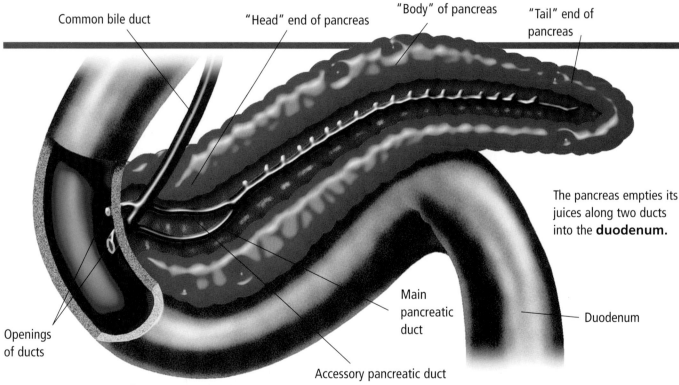

Common bile duct

"Head" end of pancreas

"Body" of pancreas

"Tail" end of pancreas

The pancreas empties its juices along two ducts into the **duodenum.**

Duodenum

Main pancreatic duct

Accessory pancreatic duct

Openings of ducts

Two main roles

The pancreas is a dual-purpose body part. In addition to making digestive juices, it also makes **hormones.** These are chemical substances that travel in the blood and control bodily processes, including **digestion** itself. In the body's other hormone-making parts, called hormonal or endocrine glands, hormones do not flow along a tube or duct. They pass directly into the blood flowing through the gland. This also happens in the pancreas, only its digestive juices pass along the pancreatic duct.

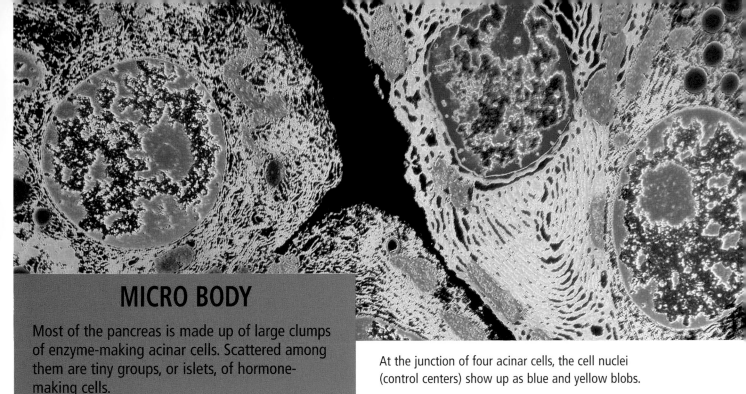

MICRO BODY

Most of the pancreas is made up of large clumps of enzyme-making acinar cells. Scattered among them are tiny groups, or islets, of hormone-making cells.

At the junction of four acinar cells, the cell nuclei (control centers) show up as blue and yellow blobs.

Ups and downs

The pancreas makes two hormones, insulin and glucagon. More insulin increases the use of **glucose,** an energy source, by microscopic **cells** all over the body. It also makes the liver convert blood glucose into body starch, which the liver stores. These two processes lower the level of glucose in the blood. Glucagon does the opposite. It tells the liver to change body starch into glucose, and it encourages conversion of various other substances into glucose, thereby raising the glucose level in the blood. The two hormones work together to adjust the blood glucose level according to the body's needs.

In diabetes, the pancreas does not produce enough insulin. Some types of diabetes are controlled by eating certain foods at certain times, and perhaps by taking pills. Other cases require injections of insulin. The condition is monitored by measuring glucose in a drop of blood by a pen-shaped device.

CHEMICALS OF DIGESTION

Enzymes

Some of **digestion** is physical. For example, the teeth bite and chew food and the stomach squeezes and churns it into a mush. But much of digestion is chemical. The main chemical substances that the body makes for digestion are called **enzymes.** They speed the attack on food to break it into smaller and smaller pieces.

Many natural processes involve enzymes. Beer is brewed by tiny microbes, yeast, whose enzymes break down sugar in the liquid.

Mouth

Enzymes begin to attack foods even before they are swallowed. **Saliva** in the mouth contains a type of enzyme known as amylase. This breaks apart food substances called starches into much smaller pieces, or sugars. This is why, as we chew starchy foods such as bread, potatoes, pasta, or rice, we can sometimes taste them becoming sweeter.

Stomach

The stomach makes two main kinds of enzymes, in addition to its powerful hydrochloric acid. Lipases attack substances called lipids in fatty foods. Pepsins work on protein food substances and split them into smaller parts known as polypeptides and amino acids.

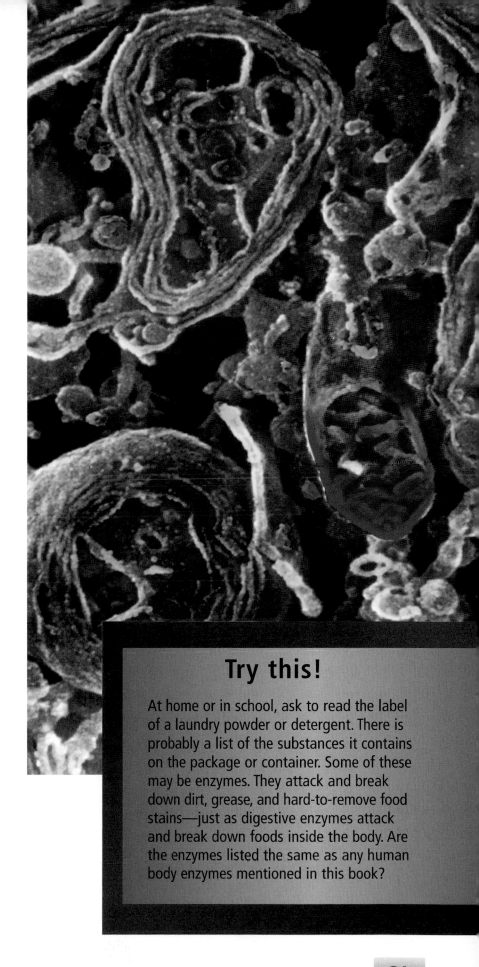

Small intestine

The small intestine receives about 15 kinds of enzymes in the juices from the pancreas. They include more amylases to attack starchy foods and lipases to digest fatty foods into smaller pieces called fatty acids and glycerols. Trypsin continues the breaking apart of protein foods into amino acids. In addition, the small intestine's lining makes about ten further kinds of enzymes to split the partially digested proteins, starches, and fats into yet smaller pieces. Finally, the breakdown products are small enough to be absorbed through the lining of the intestine and into the blood.

Deep inside a single **cell** from the lining of the small intestine are two rounded parts called lysosomes (upper center and lower left, colored blue). They make enzymes that break down the **nutrients** absorbed into the cell into smaller, simpler substances. (The yellow object at the lower right is a cell part called a mitochondrion, which provides energy.)

Try this!

At home or in school, ask to read the label of a laundry powder or detergent. There is probably a list of the substances it contains on the package or container. Some of these may be enzymes. They attack and break down dirt, grease, and hard-to-remove food stains—just as digestive enzymes attack and break down foods inside the body. Are the enzymes listed the same as any human body enzymes mentioned in this book?

Need for coordination

Digestion seems simple. We chew and swallow food—and that is it. But inside the body, the **digestive system's** many parts must work at the right times, in a coordinated way. Part of this control is carried out by **nerve** signals from the **brain.** The signals come from the lower, or "automatic" parts of the brain, so we are not aware of them. They travel mainly along the vagus nerve, which has branches to the stomach, intestines, liver, and pancreas.

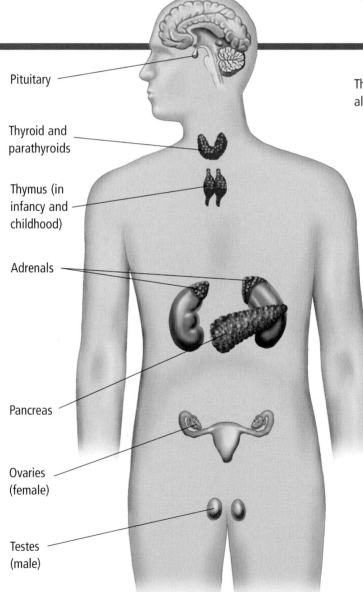

Pituitary

Thyroid and parathyroids

Thymus (in infancy and childhood)

Adrenals

Pancreas

Ovaries (female)

Testes (male)

The body's "chief" hormonal gland, the pituitary, is also one of the smallest glands.

Hormones and digestion

The body chemicals called **hormones** (see pages 28–29) also control digestion. Gastrin, from the stomach lining, makes the lining release acids and **enzymes** and starts **peristalsis** in the small intestine. Three other hormones are made by the small intestine lining. Secretin and CCK (cholecystokinin) make the liver and gallbladder empty their digestive juices into the small intestine and tell the stomach to stop releasing acid. GIP (gastric inhibitory peptide) also reduces stomach acid and calms the stomach's churning movements as food leaves it.

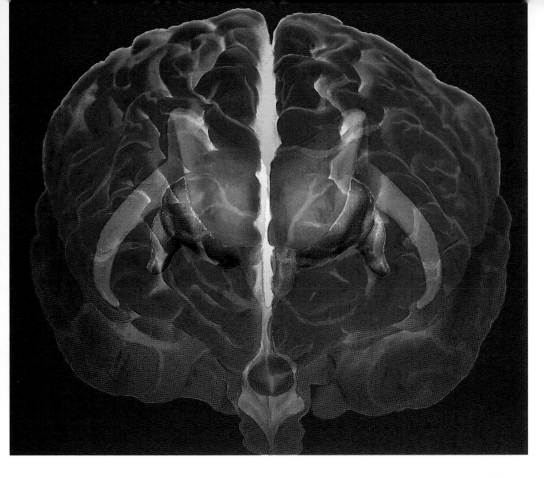

This medical scan of the brain, seen from the front, shows the pituitary as a greenish oval near the bottom of the picture. It is linked by a long stalk to a part of the brain called the hypothalamus, shown in pale green near the center. The large pink regions are the fluid-filled chambers, or ventricles, deep inside the brain.

Other hormones

Dozens of other hormones control many body processes. The adrenal glands, just above the kidneys, make the hormone epinephrine, which prepares the body for action by increasing heartbeat and breathing rates and blood flow to muscles. The thyroid gland in the neck produces thyroxine, which affects the general rate of metabolism (body chemistry). The tiny **pituitary gland,** just under the brain, makes about ten hormones. Several of these control production of other hormones elsewhere, which is why the pituitary is known as the "chief hormonal gland." The pituitary also produces the growth hormone that affects the body's growth from baby to adult.

ANIMAL VERSUS HUMAN

The axolotl is a rare kind of salamander from Mexico. Its lake water lacks the **nutrients** needed to make certain hormones, which means the axolotl "never grows up." It has the body of an adult salamander but keeps the frilly gills that other salamanders lose as they become adults.

THE THIRSTY BODY

The need for water

Imagine it is a hot day and you are playing sports in the sun. The body will be losing lots of water in sweat. It is very important to replace this water by taking in plenty of liquids. If the level of water in the body falls too low, a condition known as dehydration, then body parts begin to suffer, including the muscles, heart, and **brain.**

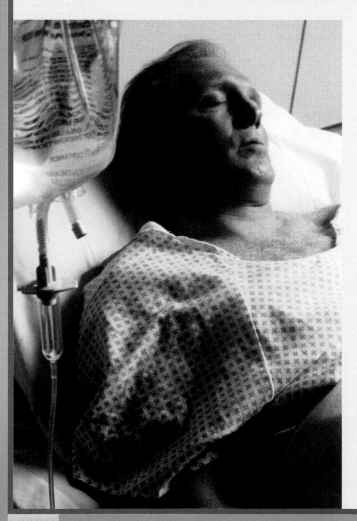

Water balance

The whole body is almost two-thirds water. Controlling the amounts in different body parts is vital for health, strength, and clear thinking. Water moves around and is "recycled" inside the body in many different ways, so that we do not have to drink huge amounts. For example, each day **digestion** produces over ten quarts (less than ten liters) of watery products, such as **saliva** and the juices from the stomach, pancreas, and small intestine. But most of this liquid is taken back into the body, mainly in the large intestine.

A hospital patient receives vital fluids from a bag through a tube, which connects to a needle inserted into a **vein** in the forearm. Lack of fluids for just a few hours can endanger life.

Top Tips

When the body starts to feel very thirsty, it is already too short of water. It is wise to avoid the feeling of thirst by taking small drinks regularly. This is better than one huge drink, which can sometimes cause nausea (feeling sick) or even vomiting.

Hormonal control

The amount of water lost by the body in **urine** is mainly under the control of **hormones** (see page 28). One of the main hormones is ADH (antidiuretic hormone), made in the adrenal glands, one above each kidney. When the body's water level falls, more ADH is released, and it causes the kidneys to produce urine with the same amount of wastes but less water. This is why, on a hot and sweaty day, the body saves water by producing only small amounts of urine. On a cold day and after plenty of drinks, the amount of urine is much larger. Under average conditions, every day the body loses about 3.5 ounces (100 milliliters) of water in **feces** and 40–50 ounces (1,200–1,500 milliliters) in urine.

Water in foods

Water in sweat and breath

Metabolic water (water made by body chemistry)

WATER IN

WATER OUT

Water in drinks

Water in urine

Water in feces

On average, the body loses as much water as it gains each day, mainly by adjusting the amount of water leaving in urine.

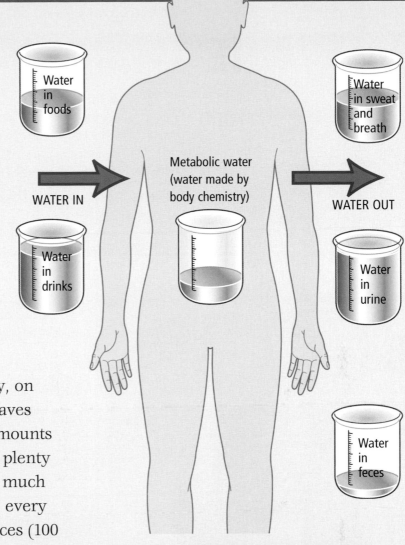

Clumps of hormone-making **cells**

The adrenal gland has two distinct layers, the outer cortex and inner medulla, that produce very different hormones.

Capsule (outer covering)

Cortex

Medulla

Base of gland sits on top of kidney

THE LYMPH SYSTEM

Fluid and tubes

The main place for absorbing digested **nutrients** is the small intestine. This is covered with tiny "hairs," called **villi,** shown earlier (page 21). Nutrients pass into the blood in the microscopic vessels called **capillaries,** inside each villus. The blood flows to the liver and around the body.

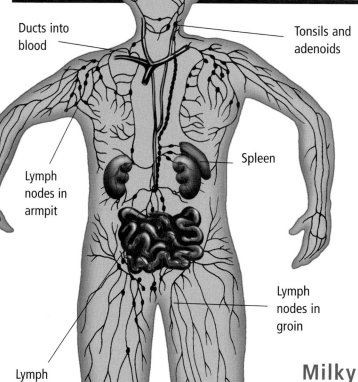

Ducts into blood

Tonsils and adenoids

Lymph nodes in armpit

Spleen

Lymph nodes in groin

Lymph nodes from intestines

The lymph system gathers fluid from the intestines and many other body parts and adds it into the blood system through the main **veins** in the chest.

Another specialized liquid inside each villus also takes up digested nutrients, especially fats. It is **lymph,** and it is collected in each villus by a tiny tube. Lymph from millions of lacteals in the small intestine collects in wider tubes, lymph vessels, that join into the general network of lymph vessels throughout the body.

Milky fluid

The average body contains one to two quarts (about one to two liters) of lymph fluid. In some ways it is similar to blood—it flows through tubes, carries many important substances around the body, and collects wastes. However, lymph is milky-looking rather than red. Also, it is not contained in tubes for all of its journey. It begins as general "body fluid" around and between the billions of **cells** in all body parts. This fluid oozes slowly, pushed along by the squeezing action of muscles as the body moves around, since, unlike blood, lymph does not have its own pump.

Back into the blood

All around the body, lymph fluid gradually makes its way into the open ends of lymph vessels. These join together and become wider, and, along with the lymph vessels from the intestines, lead into the upper chest. Here, the largest lymph vessels join to main blood vessels just above the heart. In this way the lymph fluid, rich in nutrients from the intestines and also waste substances from all over the body, becomes part of the blood.

Lymph lumps

Along lymph vessels there are small, lumpy enlargements known as **lymph nodes.** These occur especially in the neck, armpits, lower **abdomen,** and groin area between the legs. The nodes are packed with white blood cells that fight germs, as shown on the next page.

MICRO BODY

Lymph nodes are packed with many kinds of cells that attack microbes and fight disease.

Cells gathered inside a lymph node include lymphocytes (pink), which are a type of white blood cell, and macrophages (light brown), which surround and engulf germs and other unwanted items.

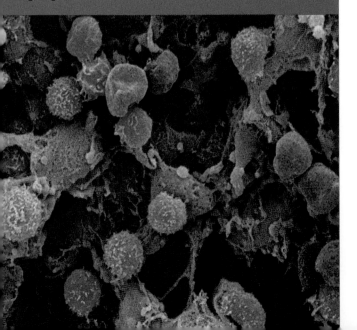

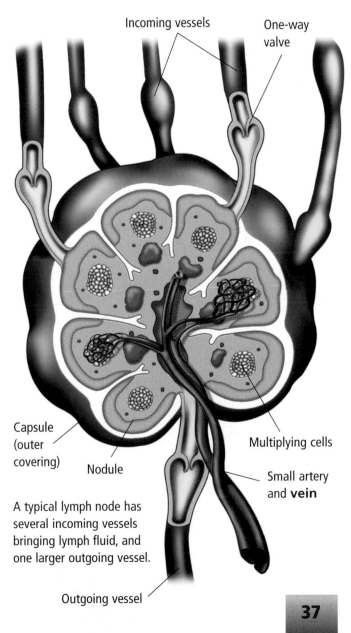

Incoming vessels

One-way valve

Capsule (outer covering)

Nodule

Multiplying cells

Small artery and **vein**

A typical lymph node has several incoming vessels bringing lymph fluid, and one larger outgoing vessel.

Outgoing vessel

FIGHTING GERMS

Defending the body

Cleanliness is very important for a healthy **digestive system.** Washing hands, using clean plates and silverware, preparing and cooking food in a hygienic way, and ensuring that water is fresh and clean all reduce the chances that harmful microbes or germs will get into the body. Microbes taken into the digestive system are usually killed by the powerful hydrochloric acid and **enzymes** in the stomach and intestines. But sometimes they survive, in which case they are attacked by the body's defense system. Microbes that get in by other routes, such as through a cut in the skin, or in breathed-in air, are also attacked by this body system.

The immune system

The body parts that defend against attack by microbes, and against illness and disease in general, together are known as the **immune system.** Its main parts include **lymph nodes** (see page 37), the tonsils in the back of the throat, and the spleen in the upper left **abdomen.** They are packed with microscopic white **cells,** which can change shape and move to where germs are most numerous. White cells surround and "eat" germs, or make substances known as antibodies that stick to the germs and kill them.

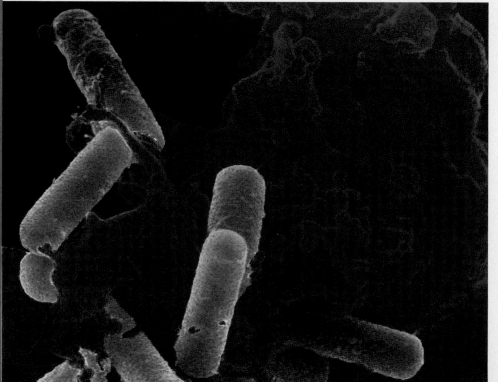

A relatively large white blood cell called a phagocyte (orange) extends its many complex arm-like "tentacles" around rod-shaped bacterial germs (blue), ready to engulf them.

Top Tips

A varied and balanced **diet** helps to keep the body healthy so that it can fight off illness and infection more effectively. In particular, lack of **vitamins** (see pages 44–45) can weaken the immune system so that germs are able to invade and multiply more easily. This is why eating vitamin-rich foods regularly, especially fresh fruits and vegetables, is so important.

Swollen glands around the face and neck are enlarged lymph nodes and may signify that the body is fighting an infection by germs. The doctor feels for swellings and tender areas during an examination.

Immunization

The germs from some diseases can be killed or made inactive and then be put into the body to make the body fight against them but without suffering the disease. This is called immunization, or vaccination. Then, if the real germs try to attack in the future, the body can recognize them and kill them very quickly.

When parts of the body suffer from disease, the lymph nodes in those areas become full of white cells, dead germs, and lymph fluid. The lymph nodes may swell and become painful. They are then known as "swollen glands."

BODY WASTES

Solid wastes

The human body produces several kinds of wastes and unwanted substances, and they leave in various ways. One example is carbon dioxide, which is made from the breakdown of **glucose** for energy, and which is removed in breathed-out air. A more obvious waste is the leftover and undigested foods removed from the end of the digestive tract. They are called **feces,** bowel movements, or solid wastes.

Importance of fiber

On average, 5.5–7 ounces (150–200 grams) of feces leave the tract each day. Two-thirds is water. The rest is a mixture of undigested food, **cells** rubbed off the linings of the **digestive tract,** and

billions of once "friendly" but now dead microbes, as mentioned on page 22. If a person eats plenty of the food substance called fiber, the feces are usually more bulky. This helps the large intestine to work more effectively and allows the feces to leave the end of the tract more easily, without straining. Fiber is found especially in brown rice, whole- grain breads, fruits, vegetables, and beans.

Liquid waste

Another obvious body waste is in liquid form. It is called **urine.** It comes from a storage bag, the bladder, in the lower **abdomen.** It leaves the bladder along a tube, the **urethra,** that carries it to the outside. The action of emptying urine from the bladder is known as urination. The bladder of an adult person typically holds 10–13.5 ounces (300–400 milliliters) of urine before its owner feels the urge to empty it. It can hold more, but this causes increasing discomfort and the feeling to empty the bladder becomes very urgent. The way that urine is produced is shown on the next page.

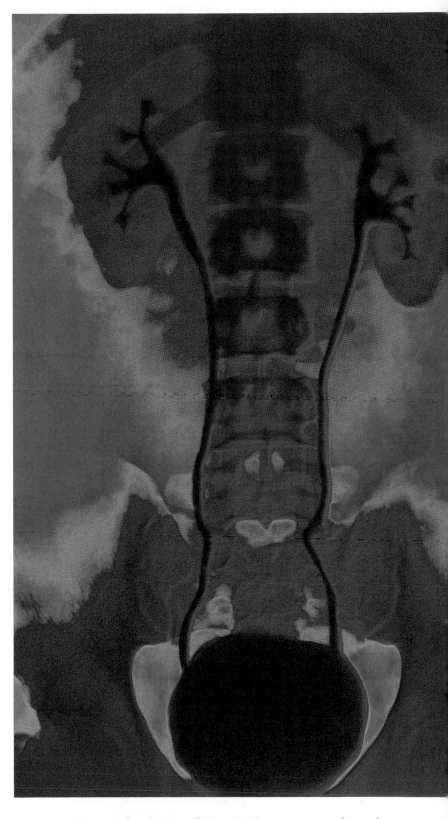

The specialized X-ray called an IVP (intra-venous pyelogram) shows the urine formed by the two kidneys and the tubes, called ureters, leading down to the bladder.

The kidneys

The body's liquid waste, **urine,** is produced by the excretory or urinary system—the kidneys, ureters, bladder, and **urethra.** The kidneys are bean-shaped organs, each about four inches (eleven centimeters long). They are in the upper rear of the **abdomen,** one on either side. In most people the left kidney, which is behind the stomach, is slightly higher than the right one, which is behind the liver.

Blood flows to each kidney along the renal artery and away again through the renal vein. These blood vessels are very wide for the size of the kidney itself. Urine collects in the central part of each kidney, the renal pelvis.

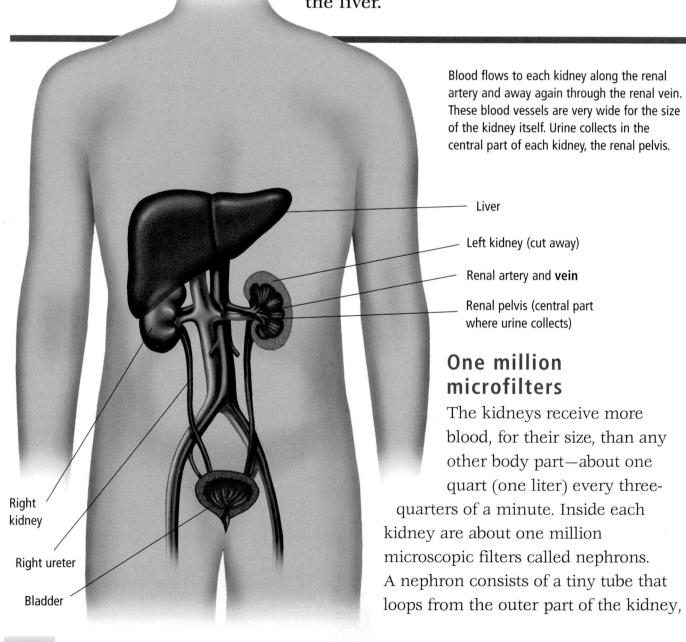

Liver

Left kidney (cut away)

Renal artery and **vein**

Renal pelvis (central part where urine collects)

Right kidney

Right ureter

Bladder

One million microfilters

The kidneys receive more blood, for their size, than any other body part—about one quart (one liter) every three-quarters of a minute. Inside each kidney are about one million microscopic filters called nephrons. A nephron consists of a tiny tube that loops from the outer part of the kidney, toward its center, and then back again. The start of the tube, called the glomerular capsule, is shaped like a cup. It receives water containing both wastes and useful substances from the glomerulus, a tiny knot of **capillary** blood vessels inside the cup.

This liquid flows along the looped tube, where useful substances plus enough water for the body's needs are taken back into the blood. At the lower end of the tube the liquid, now called urine, flows into the middle of the kidney, along with urine from the other million nephrons. If all the nephron tubes in one kidney were straightened and joined, they would stretch 31 miles (50 kilometers).

Down to the bladder

Urine contains urea, certain minerals and salts, and water that the body does not need. It passes from each kidney along a tube, the ureter, down into the bladder. The ureters, like the **digestive tract,** are squashed flat by pressure inside the body, but they also have muscles in their walls to make the wavelike movements of **peristalsis.** These movements squeeze the urine down into the bladder.

MICRO BODY

Each microfilter in the kidney has a bunchlike knot of tiny blood vessels, glomerulus, from which wastes and excess water are removed and then processed to form urine.

The glomeruli in this microphotograph are colored blue by computer. The linking blood vessels are orange.

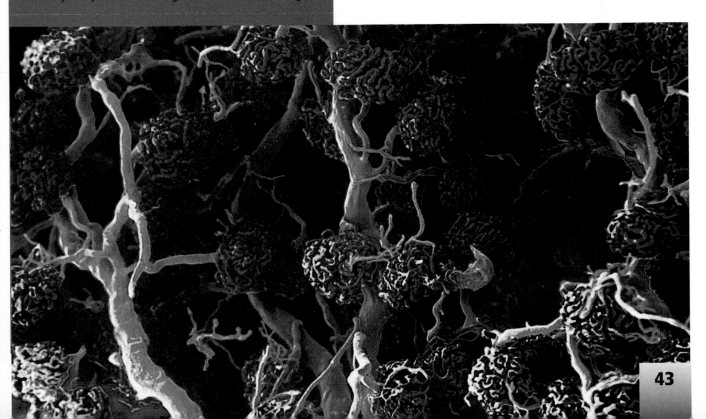

HEALTHY EATING

A balanced diet

The body needs many different kinds of foods to stay healthy. There are several main kinds of food groups or substances, and each is important for the body's needs, as is the balance between them. A healthy **diet** includes at least five portions of fresh fruits and vegetables each day.

Food and illness

Eating in an unhealthy way does not affect just the **digestive system**—it can also cause problems in many other parts of the body. For example, too many foods that are rich in animal fats can cause diseases of the heart and blood vessels. One of the most serious health problems in developed countries is obesity— being overweight due to eating too much. Obesity increases the risks of dozens of health problems, from heart disease to painful joints. The remedy is simple: Eat less and get plenty of suitable exercise.

CARBOHYDRATES
Also known as starches and sugars. Main use is for energy. Found in bread, potatoes, pasta, rice, and various fruits and vegetables.

PROTEINS
Important for body structure, to build and repair its parts. Needed especially for growth and for strong bones and muscles. Found in all kinds of meat, fish, milk, eggs, cheese, beans, and in some vegetables.

Playing sports on an empty stomach, or just after a large meal, can lead to dizziness, abdominal pain, nausea, and cramps. The body needs enough food to supply energy for activity—but not too much.

Top Tips

Many people have a rushed and hurried lifestyle. When time is short, one of the meals they are most likely to miss is the first of the day: breakfast. Yet this is also one of the most important meals. It provides a boost of energy throughout the morning and keeps the digestive system working in a regular way.

VITAMINS AND MINERALS
Used in many different ways inside the body, such as keeping the skin and **nerves** healthy, allowing the production of new microscopic **cells** for the blood, and helping the body to fight disease. Found especially in fresh fruits and vegetables and whole grains.

OILS AND FATS (LIPIDS)
Needed for several reasons, such as to provide energy and to build certain body parts such as nerves. Healthiest kinds are oils from plant products, such as vegetable oils. Eating too many fats from animal sources, such as fatty meats, is not healthy.

FIBER
This substance is not digested and absorbed by the body, but it helps the digestive system work well and reduces the risk of disorders of the **digestive tract** such as colon cancer. Found in whole-grain breads, pasta, rice, beans, fresh fruits, and vegetables.

GLOSSARY

abdomen lower part of the main body or torso, below the chest, it contains mainly the parts for digestion, excretion, and reproduction

brain incredibly complex part of the body, it is in the upper part of the head and made of billions of nerve cells and nerve fibers. The brain receives information from the senses, controls the body's movements and processes, and is the site of thoughts, memories, conscious awareness, and the mind.

capillary smallest type of blood vessel, much thinner than a human hair, with walls only one cell thick

cell single unit, or "building block," of life, the human body is made of billions of cells of many different kinds

colon large intestine

diet all of the foods and drinks that a person consumes

digestion breaking down food substances into smaller, simpler parts that can be taken into the body

digestive system parts of the body involved in taking in, breaking down, absorbing, and processing foods and the nutrients they contain

digestive tract long passageway through the body, from the mouth to the anus

duodenum first part of the small intestine, after the stomach

enamel white or whitish-yellow substance forming the very hard outer layer of a tooth

enzyme substance that breaks apart or changes another substance into different forms. There are many enzymes used in digestion and also in other body processes.

feces leftovers of the digestive process, they leave the digestive tract through the anus

glucose sugary substance, often called "blood sugar," that is found in the blood and many

body parts and is broken apart to give the body its main source of energy

hormones natural body chemicals, made by parts called endocrine glands, that circulate in blood and control many processes, such as growth, the use of energy, water balance, and the formation of urine

ileum third and last part of the small intestine, after the jejunum and before the large intestine

immune system parts that defend the body against attack by microbes and against illness and disease in general

jejunum second part of the small intestine, after the duodenum and before the ileum

lymph milky-looking fluid from around and between cells and tissues that flows into tubes called lymph vessels and eventually into the blood system

lymph node enlarged, lumplike part of a lymph vessel or tube containing millions of cells that kill germs. Lymph nodes usually swell during illness and are then known as "swollen glands."

mucus general name for various thick, slimy fluids made by the body, especially to coat and protect the surfaces of its inner parts

nerves long, thin, stringlike parts inside the body, they carry information in the form of nerve impulses, or signals

nutrients substances that the body uses in various ways, such as for growth, to build new parts and tissues, and to break apart food substances for energy and other uses

peristalsis wavelike, squeezing motion of muscles, especially where they form a tube or bag and squeeze to move along the contents

pituitary gland tiny part under the front of the brain inside the head, it makes many different hormones and controls a variety of bodily processes such as growth

saliva watery liquid made by six salivary glands inside the face, it moistens the mouth and flows onto food to help chewing and swallowing

urethra tube leading from the urinary bladder to the outside, along which the waste liquid called urine passes during urination

urine waste liquid made in the kidneys by filtering unwanted substances and water from the blood

vein blood vessel with thin walls that carries blood under low pressure back to the heart

villi tiny hair- or fingerlike projections, especially those lining the small intestine. One is called a villus.

vitamins naturally occurring substances either made by the body or taken up in food, that are needed to keep the body healthy and to avoid illness

FURTHER INFORMATION

BOOKS

Bellenir, Karen. *Diet Information for Teens: Health Tips for Teens About Diet and Nutrition.* Detroit: Omnigraphics, 2001.

Brynie, Faith Hickman. *101 Questions About Food and Digestion That Have Been Eating at You—Until Now.* Brookfield, Conn.: Millbrook Press, 2002.

Morrison, Ben. *The Digestive System.* New York: Rosen, 2000.

ORGANIZATIONS

American Association of Kidney Patients
3505 E. Frontage Road, Suite 315
Tampa, FL 33607
(800) 749-2257
www.aakp.org

American Dietetic Association
120 South Riverside Plaza, Suite 2000
Chicago, IL 60606-6995
(800) 877-1600
www.eatright.org

Children's Liver Association for Support Services
27023 McBean Parkway, Suite 126
Valencia, CA 91355
(877) 679-8256
www.classkids.org

INDEX